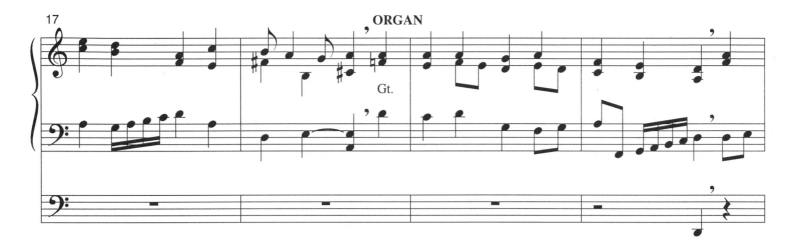

4

CANZONA
from the "Folkloric Suite"
for Organ and Brass Quartet (or Organ Solo) *

JEAN LANGLAIS
Brass adapted by
KENNETH DANCHIK

Sw. Gt. Ch. Found. st. 8' 4' 2' mixtures except Cornets
Ped.　　　　Found. st. 8' 4'
Manuals coupled. Manuals to Ped.

Allegro (♩ = 104)

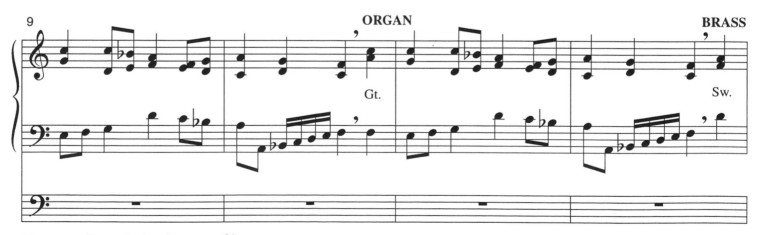

* **Brass** = play only in absence of brass;

　+ **Brass** = organ plays with brass;

　-Brass = organ only

F0648

© Copyright 1954, 2003 by H. T. FitzSimons Company. All rights reserved. Made in U.S.A.

CANZONA

from the "Folkloric Suite"
for Organ and Brass Quartet
or Organ Solo

by
Jean Langlais

Adapted by
Kenneth Danchik

H. T. FitzSimons Company

One of the Fred Bock Music Companies

EXCLUSIVELY DISTRIBUTED BY
HAL•LEONARD

Sw. add Found. st. Mixtures, Reeds 8' 4'
Ch. Krumhorn off, add Found. st. Mixtures, Reeds 8' 4'
Gt. add Found. st. 16'

ORGAN

Sw. and Ch. to Gt.
a tempo

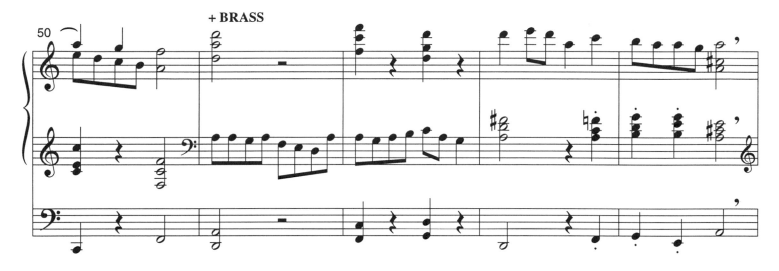

+ **BRASS**

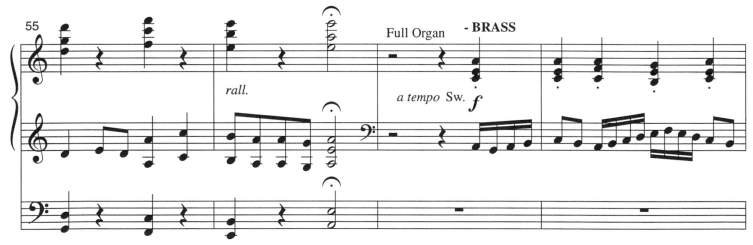

Full Organ — **BRASS**

rall.

a tempo Sw. *f*

+ **BRASS** — **BRASS**

Gt.

Sw.

B♭ Trumpet 1

CANZONA
from the "Folkloric Suite"

JEAN LANGLAIS
Brass adapted by
KENNETH DANCHIK

Permission is granted to duplicate this page.

© Copyright 1954, 2003 by H. T. FitzSimons Company. All rights reserved. Made in U.S.A.

C Trumpet 1

CANZONA
from the "Folkloric Suite"

JEAN LANGLAIS
Brass adapted by
KENNETH DANCHIK

Permission is granted to duplicate this page.

© Copyright 1954, 2003 by H. T. FitzSimons Company. All rights reserved. Made in U.S.A.

Bb Trumpet 2

CANZONA
from the "Folkloric Suite"

JEAN LANGLAIS
Brass adapted by
KENNETH DANCHIK

Permission is granted to duplicate this page.

© Copyright 1954, 2003 by H. T. FitzSimons Company. All rights reserved. Made in U.S.A.

C Trumpet 2

CANZONA
from the "Folkloric Suite"

JEAN LANGLAIS
Brass adapted by
KENNETH DANCHIK

Permission is granted to duplicate this page.

© Copyright 1954, 2003 by H. T. FitzSimons Company. All rights reserved. Made in U.S.A.

Trombone 1

CANZONA
from the "Folkloric Suite"

JEAN LANGLAIS
Brass adapted by
KENNETH DANCHIK

Permission is granted to duplicate this page.

© Copyright 1954, 2003 by H. T. FitzSimons Company. All rights reserved. Made in U.S.A.

TROMBONE 2

CANZONA
from the "Folkloric Suite"

JEAN LANGLAIS
Brass adapted by
KENNETH DANCHIK

Permission is granted to duplicate this page.

© Copyright 1954, 2003 by H. T. FitzSimons Company. All rights reserved. Made in U.S.A.

EXCLUSIVELY DISTRIBUTED BY
HAL•LEONARD® CORPORATION
7777 W. BLUEMOUND RD. P.O. BOX 13819 MILWAUKEE, WI 53213

U.S. $12.95
ISBN 0-634-06453-3
ISBN-13: 978-0-634-06453-1
Distributed By
HAL LEONARD

08739717